Changing
Clothes

Claire Llewellyn

SIMON & SCHUSTER

LONDON • SYDNEY • NEW YORK • TOKYO • SINGAPORE • TORONTO

First published in Great Britain in 1991
by Simon & Schuster Young Books

Reprinted in 1994

Simon & Schuster Young Books
Campus 400
Maylands Avenue
Hemel Hempstead, Herts HP2 7EZ

© 1991 Simon & Schuster Young Books

Photographs: ZEFA except *cover*
courtesy Benetton, page 7 courtesy Next Directory,
pages 8, 14, 17TL, 22 Sally & Richard
Greenhill and page 29 Topham.

Printed and bound in Singapore
by Kim Hup Lee Printing Co. Pte Ltd

Contents

07580

Favourite clothes

We all like clothes which look good and feel comfortable.

Which are your favourite clothes?
When do you wear them?
Do you know anyone else who wears clothes like yours?

8

Buying clothes

Clothes in shops are expensive.
You need to buy just the right things.

What should people think about
when they buy clothes?   What
questions might they ask?

Second-hand clothes

People often give clothes away.
Can you think of some reasons why?

Second-hand clothes are cheaper
than new ones.   Do you know where
you can buy them?

50 P.

11

12

Clothes to keep you cool

You don't need to wear thick clothes when it's hot.

What do you wear in the summer?
What do you wear on your head and your feet?

What clothes do people in hot countries wear to keep them cool?

Clothes to keep you warm

In very cold countries people wear
thick clothes made of wool or fur.
These help to keep them warm.

What do you wear in very cold weather?
How do you keep your head,
hands and feet warm?

14

15

Clothes can keep you clean

All these people are wearing special clothes to keep them clean and dry.

What are they doing?   What would happen if they didn't wear these special clothes?

Do you ever wear clothes like these? When?

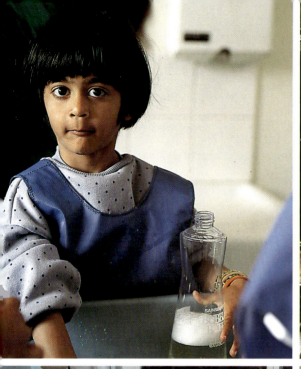

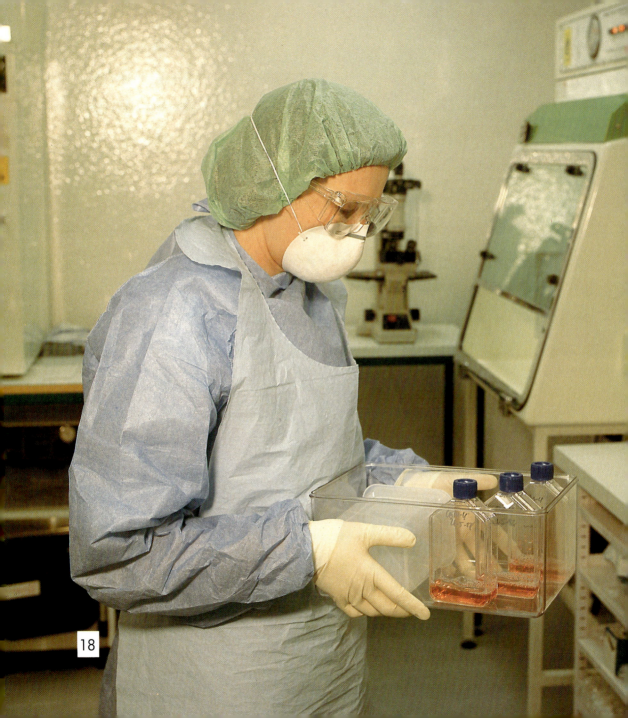

Protective clothing

The people in these pictures are wearing special clothes.   What are they doing?   How do their clothes protect them?

Can you think of any other people who wear protective clothing?

20

Uniforms can be useful

Some clothes make it easy for us to recognise people.   When might this be useful?

Can you think of anyone else who wears a uniform for work?

Clothes for school

Many children have to wear a uniform to school.   Why do you think this is? Can you think when a uniform might be useful?

Other children can wear their own clothes to school.   What do you wear?

23

24

Clothes to move around in

Look at the clothes these dancers are wearing.   Do you think they are comfortable?   Why?

Think about the times when you move around very quickly.   What do you wear?   Are your clothes comfortable?

Clothes for special days

We wear our very best clothes to parties or weddings, or perhaps at Hannukah, Diwali, Eid or Christmas.

Which are the special days in your family?   What do you wear?   How do you feel in your best clothes?

Clothes your grandparents wore

Clothes change.   These are the clothes
your grandparents might have worn
when they were young.

Ask your grandparents if they have
any old photos which show the clothes
they used to wear.

Are they like the clothes in the picture?

29

Index